THE
JOURNEY
CONTINUES
STORIES OF A SURVIVOR

THE
JOURNEY
CONTINUES
STORIES OF A SURVIVOR

by:

SIAH B. HAGIN

VINE
PUBLISHING

Published by Vine Publishing, New York, NY.

Vine Publishing books may be purchased through booksellers or by contacting:
447 Broadway,
2nd Floor, #137,
New York, NY 10013

www.vinepublish.com

ISBN: 978-0-9856535-5-2 (hardcover)
ISBN: 978-0-9856535-7-6 (paperback)
ISBN: 978-0-9856535-6-9 (e-book)

Library of Congress Control Number: 2018944763

Printed in the United States of America

THE WEIGHT

When you realize the weight of your assignment
It humbles you
You understand that your pain was an experience
To be shared
A reminder of what you have been delivered from
And who has delivered you
So you share
So that others may be healed
You expose yourself
To aid in someone's deliverance
You become uncomfortable, as it is not easy
But this is the weight of your assignment
Your assignment humbles you
It drives you to dare to believe that someone needs to
hear your story
So that they can be mended and encouraged
to share their story of survival with someone else
That is the weight of the assignment.

This book is dedicated to every individual who has experienced trauma or loss. May this book bring comfort and give you strength through your journey.

CONTENTS

FOREWORD

T*he Journey Continues: Stories of a Survivor* is exactly what's needed right now. In a social media world where we curse Mondays and post melodramatic reactions to meaningless daily occurrences, it is refreshing to read about relatable real-life challenges, and ways to overcome them from the perspective of an educated black woman!

As a father raising a beautiful and intelligent woman, it was transformative to take a glimpse into the challenges and the level of reflectiveness that women transition through. It's been my first instinct to raise her to be "tough" so she can be self-sufficient and avoid adopting any characteristics of being anyone's victim. Siah Hagin helped me to understand the nuances and various lenses that my daughter may experience throughout her life. Topics like divorce, abuse grievance, family secrets, etc. are discussed and shines light on the need for establishing a sense of empathy, self-awareness, perseverance and resilience as powerful weapons to reach your full potential. This collection of poetic stories is a well written therapeutic experience that will stay with you and challenge how you prioritize and expend emotions.

— *Ryan T Branch,*
Principal, Community Voices Middle School

INTRODUCTION

I began to write many years ago to help me on my healing journey. There were things that I needed to get out of my head and on paper, so they would stop playing in my mind. Writing became cathartic—it provided the psychological and emotional release needed in my healing process. Eventually, writing my thoughts down led to writing poetry. I guess one could say I journaled my way to healing.

When I began to write poetry, I never thought that one day I would be sharing these thoughts with others. They were personal, between God and me. They were my thoughts - my journey, my stories with a poetic rhythm. They were private, at times emotional, and other times resolute. They were deep and personal, and as I penned these poems, at no point did I ever think that they would be exposed to the world...but God knew. I have come to understand that God often has a different plan than the one we have for our lives.

Each one of us has our own journey, our own stories—stories of survival, triumph and victory. This is a collection of my stories told through poetry. As a survivor, it is my hope that these stories will represent the voice of every individual who has experienced abuse, whether emotional, physical, or sexual. It is my prayer that these stories will shine a light in dark places—expose what has been hidden, and give courage to those who have been afraid.

SPECIAL NOTE TO THE READER

After each poem, there are a few **Thought-Provoking Questions**, or **TPQs.** These are questions for you to ponder as you embark on your own journey. As you give thought to these TPQs, you might want to add your own questions and write down your feelings about what you just read. Feel free to use the space indicated as "Your Thoughts." I cannot adequately express the importance of writing. Writing is the release of a burden—a weight that no longer has to be carried, and a door that is finally closed. It allows you to let go of something that you have carried far too long. It frees the heart and mind to dream, live, love and hope once again.

Let this book be a reminder that you are not alone. Use this book as a tool—a path towards your healing, and a gift of peace.

DAMAGE

The hurt from a divorce, the haunting memories from that abuse...Damage. The demeaning words spewed from that so called "loved one" that plays over and over in your head like a recording...Damage.

Left helpless, hopeless and lost in despair. Damage causes you to question who you are. Things that used to come with ease now become a difficult task. Damage robs us of our self-worth. It whispers, "You are not good enough." It steals your bliss and leaves you vacant.

To feel damaged is to live in constant and continuous insufficiency. When you are insufficient, every aspect of your life is affected. It changes your outlook on life: how you view others, and your interpretation of how others view you.

Although damage can be crippling, it is not permanent. Just as life beats us down, it also offers hope for all of us. Find your way through damage and journey on to peace.

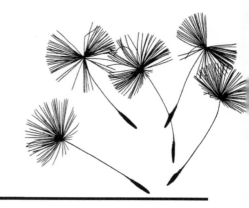

THE JOURNEY CONTINUES...

She hides her fears, cries many tears not understanding
who, how, what has gotten her here...

SOMETHING HAPPENS TO A WOMAN

Something happens to a woman

Who has been manipulated, mistreated

Abused and abandoned.

What happens to this woman?

She carries the weight of the world all on her own.

Something happens to a woman

Who has been beaten down by the turmoil of life's hand

And numb to the pain, she suffers from those who proclaimed they loved her.

What happens to this woman?

She hides her fears, cries many tears not understanding who, how, and what has gotten her here...

Here in this place of loneliness, emptiness and despair.

Something happens to a woman

A woman who has endured torment,

grief and years of pain.

What happens to this woman?

Her tears flow like a stream

Her heart bleeds for peace

Her soul is torn apart

And her mind seeks relief.

TPQs

- What life experiences have caused you to be physically and emotionally scarred?
- Have you shared these difficult times with someone you trust?
- Do you believe that there anything that can make you feel whole again?

YOUR THOUGHTS:

_____

_____

_____

_____

_____

_____

_____

_____

_____

_____

_____

_____

Aren't you older now? Why you talking about that for, anyway?

FAMILY SECRETS

Shhhh!!!!!!... HUSH!!!!!! They say
Don't say a word
Hush your mouth, don't say that
Don't talk about it, don't you DARE
It's OUR secret, family business
What uncle and cousin did,
we will NEVER tell
Why talk about it NOW they say
Don't think about it,
don't you give it another thought
Aren't you older now?
WHY YOU TALKING ABOUT THAT
FOR, ANYWAY?
Shhhhhhhh!!!!!! HUSH!!!!!!!!!!!

Child, please, GET OVER IT
Don't you know that's family business?
Listen to your FAMILY,
as they disregard your pain, and offer
no hope to alleviate your shame
As you sit and ponder, you can't help but think
Just how many family secrets have been SILENCED
and SWEPT away
Shhhhh... HUSH!!!!!!!

TPQs

No one likes to talk about the elephant in the room. Family secrets can be that big elephant in the room that everyone sees but does not speak about. This can damage a family.

- What secrets lie within your family that have caused you or others pain?

- Have these secrets caused dissention and discord within your family?

- What would happen if these secrets were exposed? How different would your family be?

YOUR THOUGHTS:

_____

_____

_____

_____

_____

_____

_____

_____

_____

_____

_____

_____

That became the prison...the trap that you live in.

THE DIVORCE

The union, the commitment, the promise
The vows that you took
Before God, loved ones and friends
That became the prison,
the trap that you live in
Waking up to...How did I get here?
Where did it go wrong?
How can I fix this?
Is it too late or is it all gone?
The guilt, anger, denial, hurt and shame
The joy turned ugly
The promise that led to pain
The union, the commitment, the promise...
the vows that you took
Where do I go from here?

TPQs

Divorce is similar to death. When one experiences a loss, it causes one to grieve. Divorce is a loss—a marriage has died, and grief is inevitable.

- What relationship commitments have you made that did not turn out the way you thought?

- How has this failed relationship affected you?

- How have you tried to deal with the disappointment in order to move forward?

YOUR THOUGHTS:

_____

_____

_____

_____

_____

_____

_____

_____

_____

_____

_____

_____

Weighed down with what we can't mend, change or control.

BURDENS

Why do we worry about the things we can't control?
Why do we hold on and refuse to let go?
Carrying other folks' stuff
Knowing it's not our own
The hurt, anger and frustration is not ours to bear
For these burdens are not to be shared
So why do we insist?
Weighed down with what we can't mend,
change or control
Learn to let go
Alleviate and release what does not belong to you
'cause I have my cross to carry and you have yours
and there is no capacity to carry burdens
that are not our own

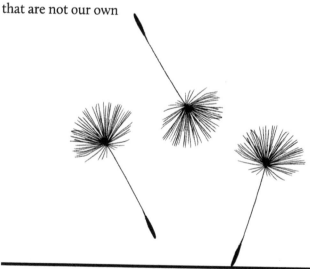

TPQs

At times we seem to take on the weight of the world. We worry about what we can't control and carry burdens that are not our own.

- Do you often worry about other people's responsibilities?
- What burdens do you carry that belong to others?
- What impact has this had on you?

YOUR THOUGHTS:

_____

_____

_____

_____

_____

_____

_____

_____

_____

_____

_____

_____

STRUGGLE

To struggle is to be human. Life and struggles go hand in hand and in fact, I believe that we are reminded of how alive we are when we go through difficult circumstances. Struggles are a part of life. Some struggles are easier to overcome while others knock us off our feet. Many of us struggle to hold on to our faith when our circumstances don't seem to be changing. At times we struggle to be hopeful when our heart tells us things can't get any better. As I started my journey towards healing I struggled with believing that I could ever get to a place of wholeness. I doubted myself and my ability to survive through it all. It was a daily struggle, and I had to make a decision to take it one day at a time. You have to make a decision to take it one day at a time. I know, to struggle does not feel good, but it reminds us of how strong we are. Struggle is uncomfortable, yet it allows us to grow in ways that we never imagined.

Life is filled with struggles but there is purpose in the struggle. Struggles show us just what we are made of. Every tear that you cry in the struggle is designed to make you stronger. Dealing with the after-effects of my abuse was a struggle. It was painful and some days I was not sure if I could fully walk in my healing, but I persisted. I persisted through the most difficult times, and today I know that I am stronger for having gone through it. The joy of going through the struggle is coming out on the other side victorious. Go through the struggle.

THE JOURNEY CONTINUES...

What will happen when the darkness gives way to light?

I WAS AFRAID TO SPEAK

I was afraid to speak
I was almost afraid to let my voice be heard
To unleash the dark secrets
To speak the injustice and the pain
Those thoughts that I carried as I went about my day
and never mumbled a word
What will it feel like
when I finally give life to what has been silenced?
What will happen when the darkness gives way to light?
I was almost afraid to speak
To let my voice be heard
But once the light came forth, my voice was heard
and the darkness withered away

TPQs

Finding your voice and walking in your truth is liberating.

- Have you ever been afraid to speak your truth out of fear of being judged?
- How has your silence stunted your growth?
- What will it mean to speak your truth?

YOUR THOUGHTS:

_____

_____

_____

_____

_____

_____

_____

_____

_____

_____

_____

_____

_____

Life goes on, healing is possible.

GRIEVE

I find myself grieving
Grieving for your losses and mine
I often think not of the great things
that we have in common but of the suffering
It brings tears to my eyes to know the pain that we share
We don't ask for help,
we find comfort in depending only on ourselves
Despite having been hurt, disappointed, lied to,
betrayed, deceived, mistreated, abused...
So grieve
Grieve for your losses and mine
Grieve while smelling the roses,
while listening to the birds sing in the early morning hours
Knowing that life goes on, healing is possible
and hope is the flower that blossoms in its own time.

TPQs

Grieving is a part of life. Although it is unpleasant, it is the pathway to healing. If we don't grieve, we can't heal.

- What are the losses in your life you have yet to grieve?
- Are you having difficulty managing your feelings regarding these losses?
- As you grieve, what are the steps you can take to aid in your healing?

YOUR THOUGHTS:

_____

_____

_____

_____

_____

_____

_____

_____

_____

_____

_____

_____

_____

I am a woman , thriving and breaking the barriers set before me.

WHO DO YOU PERCEIVE ME TO BE?

Who do you perceive me to be?
What place do you think I hold in today's society?
What can I accomplish through the lenses from which
you look at me?
Who do you perceive me to be?
As a woman, living, working...thriving;
breaking the barriers set before me
I am that woman who defies the odds
I am she, who accepts the challenges and dares to dream!

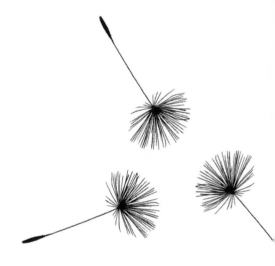

TPQs

Everyone has an opinion. They have preconceived notions and draw conclusions based on their own experiences. This becomes problematic when we allow the voices of others to cause us to question who we are.

- How have you allowed the opinions and judgments of others to affect who you are?
- Have you questioned your gifts and abilities based on someone's perception of you?
- How would your life change if you began to see yourself differently?

YOUR THOUGHTS:

_____

_____

_____

_____

_____

_____

_____

_____

_____

_____

_____

_____

_____

But it's the uncertainty, the possibility and the maybe that

tears me up inside.

THE UNCERTAINTY, POSSIBILITY AND MAYBE OF YOUR LOVE

I can be by myself
For I'm used to being alone
But I can't live with the uncertainty, the possibility, or
the maybe of being loved by you
I can eat alone, sleep alone and even vacation alone
But it's the uncertainty, the possibility and
the maybe that tears me up inside
I can live alone, for I am comfortable with myself
But the uncertainty, the possibility and
the maybe of your love; that doesn't work for me
If you are incapable of loving me
in the way that I am worthy
It is best that you leave me be
For I am used to being alone, that I can do
But the uncertainty, the possibility and
the maybe I can do without.

TPQs

Loneliness is real. The desire to be loved by others can cause us to settle for people, places and things far beneath our worth. It is important to know who you are and to understand your worth.

- Have you settled for a relationship that does not reflect your worth?
- How has this settling caused you to settle in other areas of your life?
- What are some steps that you can take to change your situation?

YOUR THOUGHTS:

_____

_____

_____

_____

_____

_____

_____

_____

_____

_____

_____

_____

You can stay the same, just as you are.

THE COMFORT ZONE

The comfort zone is where everyone wants to live
To stay safe and secure without a fret or fear
To live this life of security where change never happens
and growth will never become a reality
The comfort zone doesn't require much at all
You can stay the same, just as you are
It will never ask you to think or act differently
or to stretch beyond yourself to your destiny
The comfort zone is where everyone wants to live.
...Or do we?

TPQs

I have referred to the feeling of being uncomfortable throughout this book. It is guaranteed that if you stay in your comfort zone, you will surely never grow. Growth happens outside of your comfort zone.

- What are some things that you refuse to do because they are uncomfortable?

- How has your growth been stunted because you refuse to do these things?

YOUR THOUGHTS:

_____

_____

_____

_____

_____

_____

_____

_____

_____

_____

_____

_____

An attitude of negativity or a root of hope.

WHAT WILL YOU CHOOSE TO BIRTH?

What will you choose to birth?

Can't you see it's a choice that each one of us must make?

What will you choose?

To birth bitterness, envy or hatred,

 a seed of negativity?

Or to birth love, understanding and peace,

 a seed rooted in hope?

The choice is yours to make:

An attitude of negativity or a root of hope?

Whatever you plant will surely grow.

TPQs

Our attitude surely does determine our altitude. How we view our circumstances will determine how we respond in the present, and in the future. The same situation can have a different outcome based on how we respond.

- What type(s) of seeds have you planted in your life?
- Are they seeds of hope or seeds of negativity?
- How has your past responses played a role in your present situation?

YOUR THOUGHTS:

_____

_____

_____

_____

_____

_____

_____

_____

_____

_____

_____

_____

To decrease the noise that wishes to take over your mind.

TO PROPERLY SELF-CARE

To properly self-care
Is to learn to close some doors
To close out negativity
To decrease the noise that
wishes to take over your mind
To shut down
anyone, anything, that desires to control you
To properly self-care
Is to learn how to say NO
No to people, places and things that stunt your growth
and Yes to those who wish to see you soar
To say YES to ME
To walk the path of progress to your destiny
To properly self-care you must close some doors
to protect who you are and who you will become.

TPQs

The demands of life can leave you empty, with a great need to replenish and refuel. This is what self-care is all about.

- What do you do to replenish yourself when you feel drained?

- Do you schedule "me time" like you schedule all of the other commitments in your life?

- How can lack of self-care negatively affect your daily life?

YOUR THOUGHTS:

_____

_____

_____

_____

_____

_____

_____

_____

_____

_____

_____

_____

THE WHISPERS

I hear the whispers
the whispers, they tell lies
They say, *Who do you think you are?*
You can never accomplish that
You will never be anything
The whispers
that come to steal your joy
to rob you of your worth
To disable you of your purpose
to prevent you from reaching your potential
The whispers
Do you hear them?
All around—
That negative comment
that jealous look
The whispers, they tell lies
Can you hear them?
Trying to destroy who you are and what you can become
SILENCE your soul from the whispers.

TPQ's

The whispers represent the negative responses we receive from people and the self-defeating thoughts we tell ourselves. They can be debilitating and stop us from living our best life.

- What are some "whispers" that you have told yourself?

- How have people's negative thoughts had an impact of how you live your life?

- What are some things you can do to guard your heart and mind from "the whispers"?

YOUR THOUGHTS:

_____

_____

_____

_____

_____

_____

_____

_____

_____

_____

_____

_____

STILL A STRUGGLE

Sometimes I struggle
When I look in the mirror
Do I love the person I am?
Can I trust that I am enough—
Perfect just the way I am?
I struggle to disregard the preconceived notions
Prejudices and judgments that the world brings
Displayed in every newspaper, billboard and
social media page
It's still a struggle NOT to wish that my life was different
Although I know that IT IS life's experiences that has
helped shaped who I am
It's still hard to walk in faith
When I can't see what I've been praying for
But yet I BELIEVE, and take captive every negative thought
It's still a struggle to completely love that person
Who looks back at me
When there are days when I see more flaws than beauty
But with persistence I walk through the struggle
and oppose anything, and anyone who tries to shame who
I am
Till I reach the end of my journey to GLORY

TPQ's

Sometimes we struggle with who we are. At times we feel incapable, feeling that we are not good enough. Similar to *The Whispers*, we listen to negative thoughts from others and feed our spirits with negative things. What we listen to, what we watch, and who we talk to all plays a role in how we see the world and shape how we feel about ourselves.

- What are some areas in your life that you experience struggle?

- Are there some negative people, places and things that you have allowed to influence how you live your life?

YOUR THOUGHTS:

_____

_____

_____

_____

_____

_____

_____

_____

_____

_____

_____

_____

HEALING

On the other side of pain is healing. To be healed is to be made whole, and when we are whole we are able to live life to the fullest. Healing means, "I have overcome." Where there is healing, there is peace. Peace in knowing that the pain is over and we are free. It is liberating. When we feel damaged and are experiencing struggles, healing seems unattainable... but, we know it is possible.

Healing is oftentimes not instantaneous, but it is progressive. I realized that I was on the path to healing when the pain from my abuse did not cripple me the way it once did. Over time the pain subsided, and I slowly began to feel whole again. Healing is possible when we have a desire to be made whole. In seeking and desiring to be healed—to be made whole, we will discover a renewed determination and a drive to live a purpose-filled life. Through healing, we become determined and driven to follow our purpose. As we go after our healing with all our hearts we will begin to understand that what we have gone through is intended to make us stronger and wiser— not to destroy us, as we once thought. I know this to be true because when I began my healing journey my perspective on life and circumstances changed. At this point in the journey I can confidently say that life goes on and healing is available to everyone who seeks it.

Seek your Healing.

THE JOURNEY CONTINUES...

I will not tweak, modify, or eliminate my standards or beliefs
to meet someone else's needs.

A WOMAN OF WORTH

I am a woman of worth

A woman of Integrity

I am Strong, Independent, Self-driven, Motivated, Dynamic, Respectful, Responsible, Secure, Confident and God-fearing

I know who I am and whose I am

I know how I am to treat others and how I am to be treated

Therefore I will not tweak, modify, or eliminate

my standards or beliefs to meet someone else's needs

I choose not to live beneath my worth

I stand in faith that what I need, I will receive

I walk in my worth, and embrace who I am

I am a woman of worth.

TPQs

A woman who values herself knows her worth. Understanding your worth means that you have standards. These standards are aligned with your worth.

- What does it mean to be a person of worth?
- What standards have you established in your life?
- Why is it important to see yourself as a person of value?

YOUR THOUGHTS:

_____

_____

_____

_____

_____

_____

_____

_____

_____

_____

_____

_____

I choose to say goodbye to the hurt and pain that you gave to me.

I CHOOSE TO LIVE

I choose to live
I choose to walk with God
I choose to go with him and find serenity
I choose to live freely
Not in the prison you tried to set for me
I choose to say goodbye
To the hurt and pain that you gave to me
I choose peace, joy and liberty
I choose to walk with God
for he has great things in store for me
'cause I choose to live.

TPQs

I Choose to Live is a declaration. In spite of the hurt and pain, I will live. It is a determination. It requires a made-up mind.

- What are you determined to live for?
- What declarations do you need to make in your life "to live"?

YOUR THOUGHTS:

_____

_____

_____

_____

_____

_____

_____

_____

_____

_____

_____

_____

Take my hand and I will walk you through it all.

I AM STILL HERE

I see everything
I hear your hurt
I know what you are going through
I see the pain
But...*I am still here*
I am aware of your circumstances
For I have allowed it to be
so that you may grow
In the midst of your trouble
I am still here
My word says, I will never leave you nor forsake you
Take my hand and I will walk you through it all
For...*I am still here*
Go through this process
Journey on...
For I am with you
and I will be here through it all
Because...*I am still here*
In times of loneliness, heartache and despair
Take comfort
Knowing that I know and...*I am still here*

TPQs

Life can be brutal. It can beat us up until we feel that we have nothing left. *I Am Still Here* is a poem of faith and hope. Our faith plays a role in helping us cope and get through challenging times.

- How do you get through life's challenges?
- What keeps you from crumbling under the pressures of life?

YOUR THOUGHTS:

_____

_____

_____

_____

_____

_____

_____

_____

_____

_____

_____

_____

_____

For my hope was restored and my eyes became open again.

MY PAIN HAS PURPOSE

My Pain Has Purpose
It drove me to my knees
It attempted to paralyze me
It lingered and tried to suffocate me
My days and nights looked the same
dark, cold and dreary
But It didn't win
For my hope was restored and
my eyes became open again
to the thought of peace and new beginnings
In the midst of it all
I realized that my pain had purpose
It changed everything that
said, "I CAN'T" to "I CAN"
Now I share it's struggles to encourage others
Because I have learned
My pain has purpose

TPQs

We experience many painful things in life, but we usually don't consider our painful experiences as an important part of someone else's healing.

- How do you view your pain?
- How can your pain from the past be used to help someone else?

YOUR THOUGHTS:

_____

_____

_____

_____

_____

_____

_____

_____

_____

_____

_____

_____

You exploited my body, but it was never yours in the first place.

YOU CAN'T HAVE ME

No matter what you've done to me, you can't have me
You shredded my heart, but I am whole again
Exploited my body, but it was never yours in the first place
Manipulated me, but I'm wiser now
Hijacked my soul, but I'm reclaiming it
Made me feel dirty and ashamed, but that was a lie
Stole my innocence, but I'm taking it back
Bullied me into compliance, but I finally see the
coward you are
Twisted my self-image, but I'm learning who I am
Defiled my understanding of faith and God
but now I see the hypocrisy of your ways
Annihilated my self-worth, but I'm rediscovering
the joy of loving myself
You can't have me, you never could
For I was never yours to control

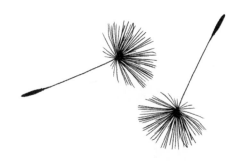

TPQs

You Can't Have Me is another poem of declaration. In order to reach the point of healing, you have to declare some things. *You Can't Have Me* is a declaration that trauma or loss will not consume you. It can't have you.

- In spite of the the trauma or loss you have experienced, you are still alive. Start your journey to healing.

- How can you make one small step toward your own declaration of "You Can't Have Me"?

YOUR THOUGHTS:

_____

_____

_____

_____

_____

_____

_____

_____

_____

_____

_____

_____

Hope rescues this woman; peace feels her grief-stricken soul.

SOMETHING HAPPENS TO A WOMAN (Reborn)

Something happens to a woman

Who has been manipulated, mistreated

Abused and abandoned

What happens to this woman?

She carries the weight of the world all on her own

Something happens to a woman

Who has been beaten down by the turmoil of life's hand

And numb to the pain she suffers from those who proclaimed they loved her

What happens to this woman?

She hides her fears, cries many tears not understanding who, how and what has gotten her here

Here in this place of loneliness, emptiness and despair

Something happens to a woman

A woman who has endured torment,

grief and years of pain

What happens to this woman?

Her tears flow like a stream

Her heart bleeds for peace

Her soul is torn apart

And her mind seeks relief

Something happens to a woman

When she encounters the Savior
Who sees her tears, feels her pain
And promises to carry the burdens life can bring
What happens to this woman?
Hope rescues this woman
Peace fills her grief-stricken soul
When she calls his name
The only one who can make her whole.

TPQs

Something Happens To A Woman appears twice in this book. It is repeated in this section in order to shine a light of hope. Despite everything this woman has gone through, she ends her journey with hope.

- What hope can you find in the rubble of life's pain?

YOUR THOUGHTS:

_____

_____

_____

_____

_____

_____

_____

_____

_____

_____

_____

_____

It breathes life in the least likely places.

HOPE FINDS A WAY

Even in the midst of death and despair
Hope Finds a Way
Through every loss and painful circumstance
In the midst of tragedy that seems to never end
Hope shines its light in the darkest alley
It breathes life in the least likely places
Hope Finds a Way
It's the light of hope, the promise of a better tomorrow
That restores, and brings peace to the soul

TPQs

Hope is powerful. It turns a dreary moment into a sunny day. It is truly that powerful. Hope reminds us that this is not the end.

- What are some things that you hope for in spite of what you have gone through?
- How does hope keep you going?

YOUR THOUGHTS:

_____

_____

_____

_____

_____

_____

_____

_____

_____

_____

_____

_____

FINAL THOUGHTS

Each one of us has a story that could easily fill the pages of this book. I am grateful for the opportunity to share mine with you, because I truly believe that what we go through should be shared to help someone else.

God has healed me through many circumstances. I have overcome the trauma of childhood sexual abuse, experienced the loss of a marriage, suffered from low self-esteem, and like many others, I have experienced the loss of loved ones. My Journey, thus far, has been filled with both joy and pain, but in the midst of it all I have learned to love me—to trust my instincts, to stand boldly on my faith, and to walk in my purpose. I am a better person as a result of my experiences. However, it is a daily walk that requires determination and much prayer. The reality is, we may feel damaged due to the afflictions of life, and we may go through struggles but we can become stronger and feel whole once again. It is my desire that you will use my expereinces to help you on your journey.

YOUR JOURNEY

This book was written to encourage and uplift—to remind you that you are not alone. I encourage you to find your voice, go through the struggles, and walk in your purpose. Most of all, begin your journey and then journey on. The journey continues...and it never ends. As long as we live, we are on a journey.

CPSIA information can be obtained
at www.ICGtesting.com
Printed in the USA
BVHW03s0246070718
521024BV00001B/4/P